19 WHY DO I BURP?

20 WHY DO PEOPLE FART?

21 WHAT IS MY TONGUE FOR?

22 WHY DO CUTS BLEED?

23 WHAT IS A SCAB FOR?

24 WHO HAS SKIN COVERED IN HOLES?

25 WHAT ARE FRECKLES?

26 WHEN DO MOLES LIVE ON PEOPLE?

27 WHAT IS A SCAR?

28 WHEN DO I NEED TO WEAR SUNCREAM?

29 WHY DO I GET GOOSEBUMPS WHEN IT'S COLD?

30 WHY DOES TICKLING MAKE ME GIGGLE?

31 WHY DO I NEED TO WASH?

32 WHAT ARE MY BONES MADE OF?

33 HOW DO MY ARMS AND LEGS BEND?

34 WHY CAN'T I TURN MY FOOT BACKWARDS?

35 WHAT WOULD HAPPEN IF I BROKE A BONE?

36 WHAT IS MY SMALLEST BONE?

37 WHAT IS MY BIGGEST BONE?

38 WHY SHOULD I BRUSH MY TEETH?

39 WHY DO TEETH GO WOBBLY?

40 WHY DO I YAWN?

41 WHAT IS SLEEP FOR?

42 WHAT AM I DOING WHEN I SLEEP?

43 WHY DO PEOPLE SNORE?

44 WHY DOES MY NOSE RUN?

45 WHAT IS A SNEEZE?

46 ARE ALL BELLY BUTTONS THE SAME?

47 WHAT MAKES ME HICCUP?

48 WHY DO SOME PEOPLE WEAR GLASSES?

49 WHAT DOES 'COLOUR BLIND' MEAN?

50 WHY DO I NEED TO GET MY NAILS CUT?

51 WHY DOES HAIR FALL OUT?

52 WHY DO EARS MAKE WAX?

53 WHAT WOBBLES INSIDE MY EAR?

54 HOW QUICKLY DOES MY HEART BEAT?

55 WHY DO I SOMETIMES GET OUT OF BREATH?

56 QUICK-QUIZ QUESTIONS

58 QUICK-QUIZ ANSWERS

60 TRICKY WORDS

62 WHERE TO FIND STUFF

64 FAREWELL

HAVE YOU EVER WONDERED WHY... OR WHAT...OR WHEN?

It's only natural to wonder about the world around us. It's a very complicated and surprising place sometimes. And you'll never understand what is going on around you unless you ask yourself a question every now and again.

We have investigated the human body to collect as many tricky questions as we could find about how your body works...

...and we also found the answers for you!

We now invite you to come with us on an exploration of the human body, so that we can show you all the answers we have discovered.

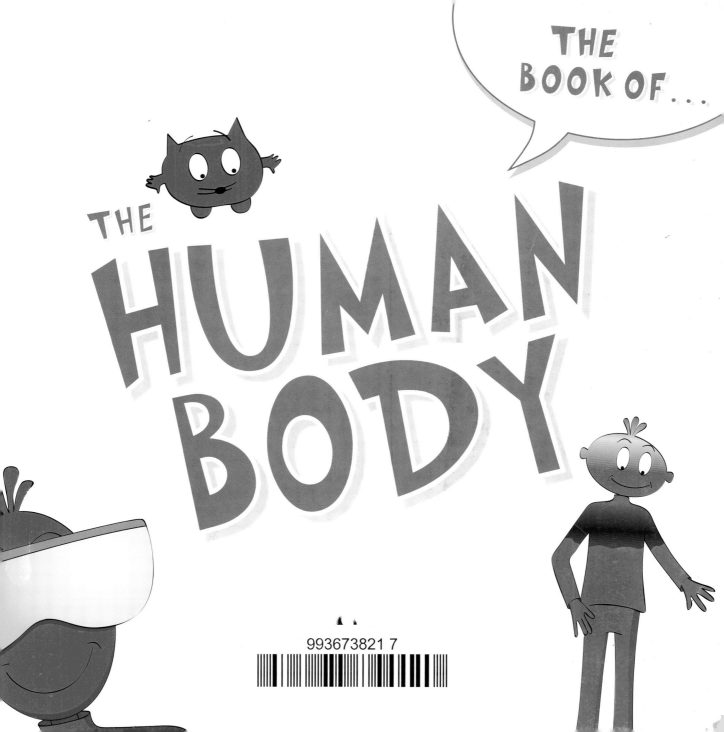

THE
BOOK OF...

THE
HUMAN
BODY

9936738821 7

 **KINGFISHER**

First published 2012 by Kingfisher
an imprint of Macmillan Children's Books
a division of Macmillan Publishers Limited
20 New Wharf Road, London N1 9RR
Basingstoke and Oxford
Associated companies throughout the world
www.panmacmillan.com

Written and Illustrated by Dynamo Limited
Concept by Jo Connor

ISBN 978-0-7534-3499-4

Copyright © Macmillan Children's Books 2012

10 9 8 7 6 5 4 3 2 1
TTR/0512/LFG/140MA

A CIP catalogue for this book is available
from the British Library.

Printed in China

WHAT'S IN THIS BOOK?

THE HUMAN BODY...

6 WHAT IS INSIDE MY BODY?

7 DO BABIES HAVE THE SAME THINGS INSIDE THEM AS ME?

8 WHY DOESN'T EVERYBODY LOOK THE SAME?

9 HOW TALL WILL I GROW?

10 WHY DO I BLINK?

11 WHY DO I CRY?

12 WHAT ARE EYEBROWS FOR?

13 IS ANYONE HAIRY ALL OVER?

14 WHY DO I GET HUNGRY?

15 WHY DO I GET THIRSTY?

16 WHY DO I POO?

17 WHAT IS WEE?

18 WHY DOES MY TUMMY RUMBLE?

We also thought it might be fun to see how much of this shiny new knowledge you can remember – so at the back of the book, on pages 56 and 57, you'll find some Quick-Quiz questions to test you out. It's not as scary as it sounds – we promise it will be fun. (And besides, we've given you all the answers on pages 58 and 59.)

While we were searching for all those answers, we found out some other pretty interesting things, too. We wrote them all down on these panels – so you can memorize these facts and impress your friends!

QUICK-QUIZ QUESTIONS

Did you know ...

Your heart beats about 100,000 times a day – that's roughly 36,500,000 beats per year!

Are you ready for this big adventure?

Then let's go!

5

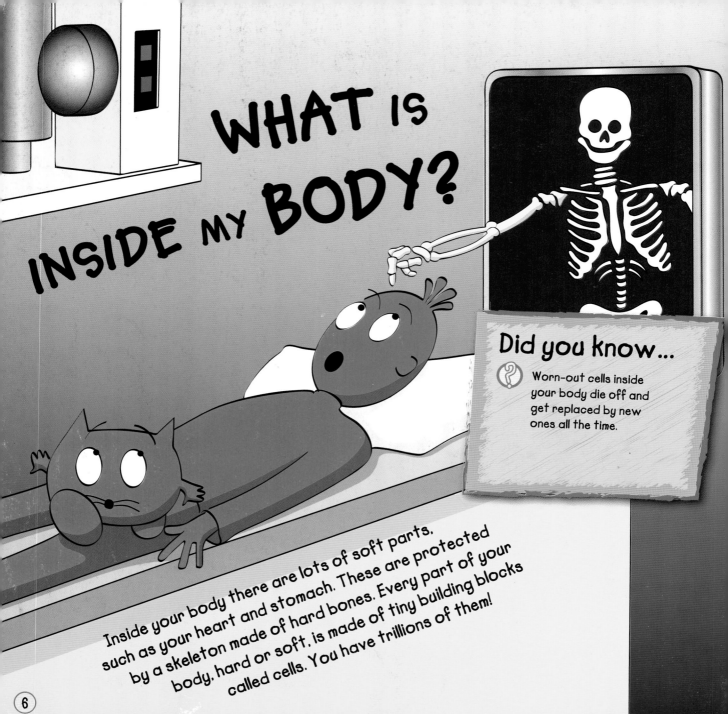

WHAT IS INSIDE MY BODY?

Did you know...

Worn-out cells inside your body die off and get replaced by new ones all the time.

Inside your body there are lots of soft parts, such as your heart and stomach. These are protected by a skeleton made of hard bones. Every part of your body, hard or soft, is made of tiny building blocks called cells. You have trillions of them!

DO **BABIES** HAVE THE SAME **THINGS** INSIDE THEM AS **ME?**

Babies are born with all the same things as children and grown-ups, only they are much smaller. Their body parts, such as their bones and brain, develop (grow and change) inside them as they get bigger. Babies grow very quickly, and double their weight in just a couple of months.

Did you know...

Your eyes stay the same size all your life, from birth to old age.

WHY DOESN'T EVERYBODY LOOK THE SAME?

Inside each one of your body cells there is a set of chemicals called DNA. Your DNA provides a kind of recipe for your body. It affects everything about you, such as how tall you will grow and how you look. Everyone has their own slightly different DNA mixture, which is why we don't all look exactly the same.

Did you know...

Your DNA is stored in tiny, ladder-shaped threads called chromosomes. Each of your body cells contains 23 pairs of chromosomes.

HOW TALL WILL I GROW?

Did you know...

Your hair grows faster than anything else on your body. It grows about 4 nanometres every second – that is about 0.4 millimetres each day.

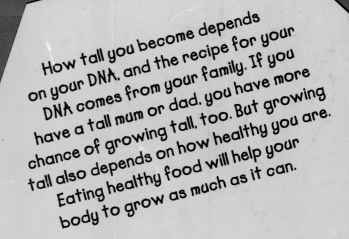

How tall you become depends on your DNA, and the recipe for your DNA comes from your family. If you have a tall mum or dad, you have more chance of growing tall, too. But growing tall also depends on how healthy you are. Eating healthy food will help your body to grow as much as it can.

WHY DO I BLINK?

You blink to stop your eyes drying out. Your top eyelids are lined with tiny body parts, called glands, that make a liquid to coat your eyes. When you blink, you spread the liquid over your eyeballs. Blinking also cleans your eye, like a windscreen wiper cleaning a car's windscreen.

Did you know...

Children and grown-ups blink between 10 and 15 times a minute, but babies blink less.

So, your top eyelids produce a liquid that cleans your eyes, but if you get upset they suddenly start to make more. Nobody knows exactly why this happens, but it may be your body's way of helping you to calm down. Tears contain a chemical called 'prolactin', which scientists think might have a calming effect.

WHY DO I CRY?

Did you know...

Your body automatically makes tears to try to clean your eyes if they are irritated by something, such as the chemicals that waft up from an onion when it is cut.

WHAT ARE EYEBROWS FOR?

Your eyebrows work like umbrellas, shielding your eyes from dirt and from the sweat that your body makes when you are hot. You can use them to show how you feel, too. We can move them down to frown or move them up to look surprised.

IS ANYONE HAIRY ALL OVER?

We have lots of tiny hairs all over our skin, to help protect it and keep it warm. Nobody is hairy all over, though. We don't have hair on the soles of our feet, the palms of our hands, our eyelids or our lips.

Did you know...

Humans have a scent, like most animals do, but it is very faint and we do not normally notice it. Our tiny hairs might help to keep it on our skin.

WHY DO I GET HUNGRY?

Your body uses food as fuel and to keep you healthy. When you need more, your brain sends you a signal that your tummy feels empty. Without food your body would eventually stop working, just as a car would stop working if it ran out of petrol.

Did you know ...

If you did not get enough food to eat, you would become thin, weak and ill.

WHY DO I GET THIRSTY?

Did you know...

Splish- splash! About two-thirds of your body is made up of water.

The feeling of thirstiness is your body's way of telling you that you need more water. Water stops your body drying out, and your body uses it to do jobs such as making blood or helping to mash up food in your stomach. You need to drink water every day to replace what you have used.

WHY DO I POO?

Your body uses some parts of the food you eat, but other parts are left over. Your body makes this into poo and pushes it out. The section of your body that takes the goodness from food and gets rid of the unwanted parts is called your digestive (dye-jest-iv) system.

WHAT IS WEE?

Did you know ...

On spacecraft such as the International Space Station, the astronauts' wee is turned back into drinking water. Their poo is collected, dried and taken back to Earth.

Wee is water mixed with waste substances that your body does not want. Its proper name is 'urine' (you-rin). It can be lighter or darker in colour, depending on what you have eaten or drunk.

WHY DOES MY TUMMY RUMBLE?

Your tummy makes special liquids called 'digestive juices', which help to break food down into different parts. The sound of a tummy rumbling is the sound of air and digestive juices being pushed around inside it. This happens most of the time – but if your tummy is empty, the noise sounds louder.

Did you know...

The medical word for tummy rumbling is 'borborygmi' (bore-bore-ig-me). The word sounds a little bit like a rumbling tummy!

WHY DO I BURP?

When you eat, you sometimes swallow air along with your food. Your body sends the air back up through your mouth as a burp. It does not harm you, but some people think that loud burps are very impolite.

Did you know...

Drinking fizzy drinks will make you burp more. They contain a bubbly gas called carbon dioxide, and your body often sends it back up as a burp.

WHY DO PEOPLE FART?

Inside your stomach, tiny organisms called bacteria help to break down the food you eat. As the bacteria work, they create gases that pass out of your body as farts. The gases are often smelly, but they are harmless.

Did you know...

On average, people fart around 14 times a day – mostly in their sleep.

WHAT IS MY TONGUE FOR?

Your tongue is covered in tiny spots called taste buds. These can sense different tastes and help you to work out what is good to eat and what is not. You taste sweet things at the front of your tongue, sour things at the back and sour or salty things at the sides.

WHY DO CUTS BLEED?

Your body has blood flowing around inside it, helping to keep you healthy. It flows through thin tubes called blood vessels. Your skin has tiny blood vessels running underneath it. So, if you cut your skin, blood leaks out from the damaged vessels.

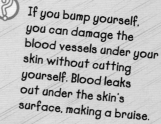

Did you know...

If you bump yourself, you can damage the blood vessels under your skin without cutting yourself. Blood leaks out under the skin's surface, making a bruise.

WHAT IS A SCAB FOR?

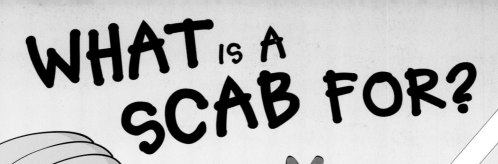

Did you know ...

A scab will fall off when the skin's surface has healed. Try not to pull it off before it is ready. Leave it to do its job!

When blood leaks out of a cut, tiny blood cells called platelets clump together to make a sticky plug called a clot. They eventually plug the hole and the clot becomes a scab that protects the cut while it heals. Underneath, your body gets busy making new skin cells.

WHO HAS SKIN COVERED IN HOLES?

Did you know...

Your hair and skin is coated in oil, made under your skin. The oil makes your skin and hair waterproof.

Everybody's skin is covered in tiny holes called pores. If you get hot your body will make sweat, a salty liquid that leaks out through the pores. It evaporates (disappears into the air), which helps to make you feel cooler.

WHAT ARE FRECKLES?

Did you know...

Freckles don't do any harm and sometimes they fade away over time. Fair-skinned people can get more freckles if they spend time outside in the sun.

Your skin has 'pigment cells' that contain the chemicals that give your skin its colour. Freckles are little clusters of pigment cells in the uppermost layer of your skin. They are most easily seen on people with fair skin.

WHAT IS A SCAR?

Did you know...

The deeper the cut, the more likely you are to get a scar, but scars fade over time.

If you ever cut your skin accidentally, your body will make new skin cells to patch it up. These new cells are slightly different to the old ones, and sometimes you can see the difference as a 'scar' mark on your skin.

WHEN DO I NEED TO WEAR SUNCREAM?

Skin burns if it receives too much sunlight, too quickly. Suncream can be worn to help filter out some of the sun's harmful effects – but it wears off after a while.

Did you know...

When skin burns in the sun, the topmost skin cells are damaged. They flake off to make way for new skin cells that move up from the skin's lower layers.

28

WHY DO I GET GOOSEBUMPS WHEN IT'S COLD?

Did you know...

Shivering is another way your body makes itself warmer when you feel cold. Your body muscles tighten and loosen quickly, to make some heat.

When you are cold, tiny muscles in your skin tighten up to make the hair on your body stand on end. This creates the little skin bumps. The bumps and the hairs trap air next to your skin, helping to keep you warm.

WHY DOES TICKLING MAKE ME GIGGLE?

Nobody knows for sure why tickling makes us laugh. It could be because your brain is surprised! Your skin contains lots of tiny nerve endings that feel touch. Some nerve endings are super-sensitive to light touching. They may signal to the brain extra-fast, and your brain reacts to the surprise by making you laugh.

Did you know...

You cannot tickle yourself. Your brain does not react to your own touch in the same way as it reacts to somebody else's touch. Perhaps this is because you cannot surprise it!

WHY DO I NEED TO WASH?

Did you know...

? As children grow into adults their skin starts to make more oil and sweat.

Your skin produces an oily coating to keep you waterproof, and salty sweat to keep you cool. If you did not wash these off sometimes, more and more dirt and bacteria would stick to the oil and sweat. You would soon start to smell and eventually become unhealthy.

WHAT ARE MY BONES MADE OF?

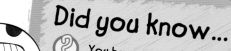
Your bones are a mixture of stretchy material and strong, hard material. They have lots of tiny holes through the middle, like a sponge, which makes them lightweight. They make up a framework inside you that keeps the shape of your body, and protects your insides.

HOW DO MY ARMS AND LEGS BEND?

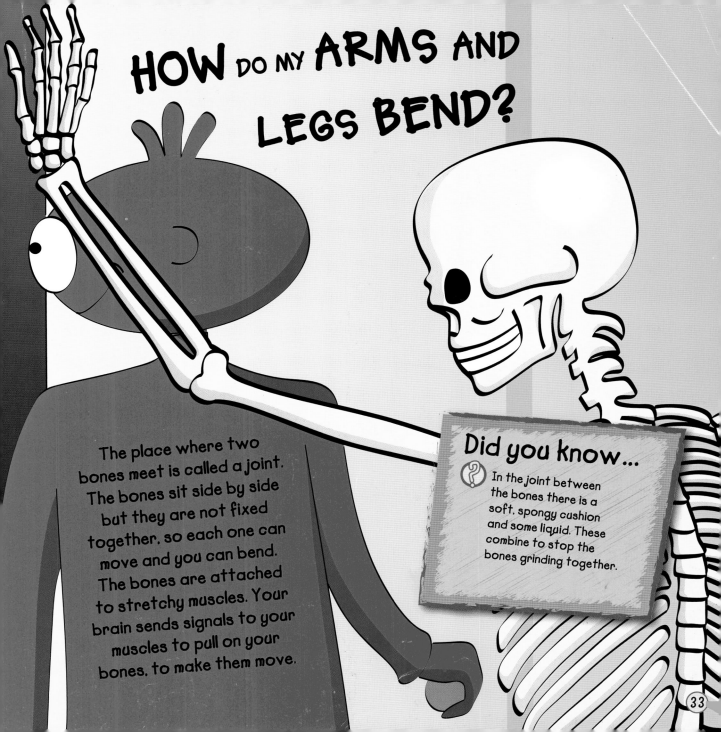

The place where two bones meet is called a joint. The bones sit side by side but they are not fixed together, so each one can move and you can bend. The bones are attached to stretchy muscles. Your brain sends signals to your muscles to pull on your bones, to make them move.

Did you know...

In the joint between the bones there is a soft, spongy cushion and some liquid. These combine to stop the bones grinding together.

WHY CAN'T I TURN MY FOOT BACKWARDS?

The way your joints are shaped fixes how your body moves, and there are differently-shaped joints in different parts of your body. For instance, the joint in your shoulder allows your arm to swing in lots of different ways, but the joint in your foot stops it turning backwards.

Did you know ...

Some people are 'double-jointed', which means they can move their joints in unusual ways and make their body more bendy than normal.

WHAT WOULD HAPPEN IF I BROKE A BONE?

Did you know...

Your bones are constantly rebuilding themselves. Old bone cells die off and new ones are made all the time.

Bones are very strong, but they can snap if they are bent too much. You could break a bone if you knocked it very hard. The bone would gradually mend itself, making new cells to knit the break together.

WHAT IS MY SMALLEST BONE?

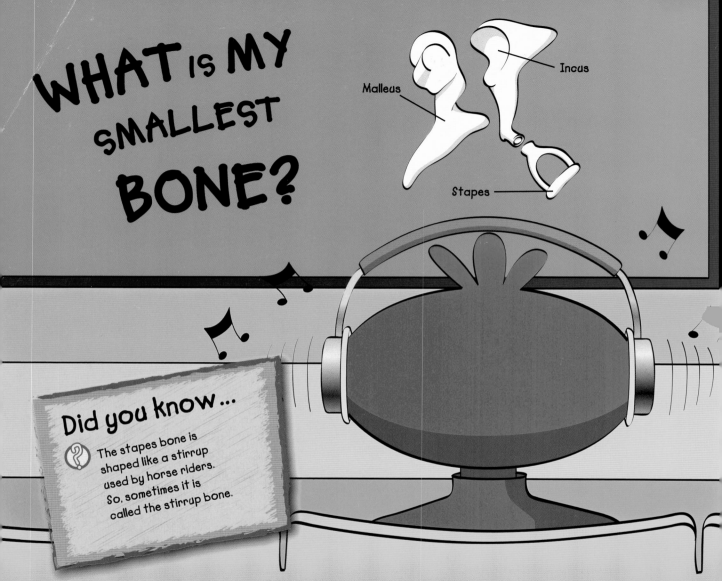

Malleus

Incus

Stapes

Did you know ...

(?) The stapes bone is shaped like a stirrup used by horse riders. So, sometimes it is called the stirrup bone.

The smallest bone in your body is inside your ear. It is called the 'stapes' (stay-peas) and it is about 3 millimetres long. Sound waves make it wobble. It passes the wobbling on to other parts of your ear, where there are nerve endings that send messages to your brain. Your brain can tell from the messages what sound you are hearing.

WHAT IS MY BIGGEST BONE?

Did you know...

Bones grow bigger all the way through childhood. They finally stop growing when a person reaches their twenties.

The longest, strongest bone in the body is the femur (fee-mer), also called the thigh bone. It is fixed between your pelvis (where your waist and hips are) and your knee. It has strong muscles fixed to it, to help you move your legs.

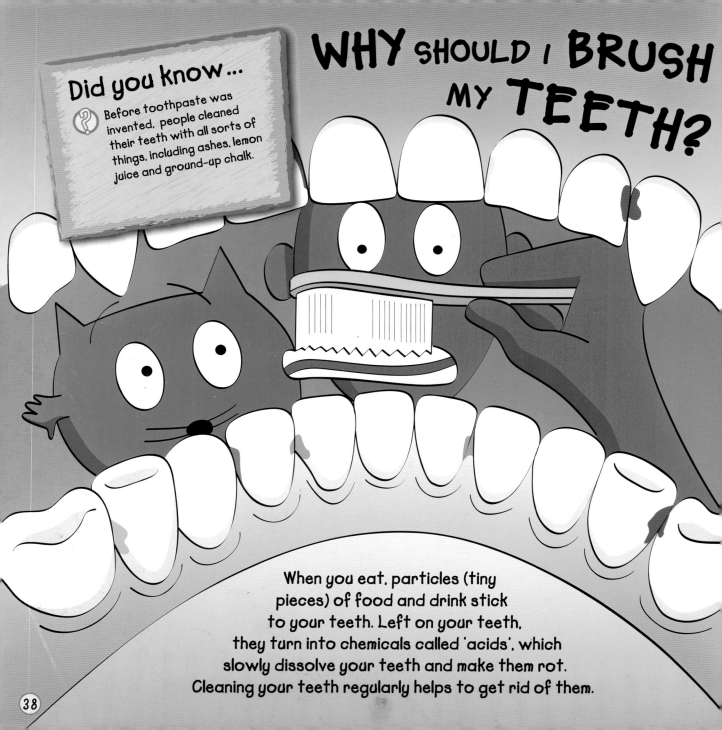

Did you know...

Before toothpaste was invented, people cleaned their teeth with all sorts of things, including ashes, lemon juice and ground-up chalk.

When you eat, particles (tiny pieces) of food and drink stick to your teeth. Left on your teeth, they turn into chemicals called 'acids', which slowly dissolve your teeth and make them rot. Cleaning your teeth regularly helps to get rid of them.

WHY DO TEETH GO WOBBLY?

Babies grow 20 small teeth called milk teeth. Then, slowly, a new set of 32 teeth grows underneath them. The first teeth go wobbly when they are being pushed out by the new teeth.

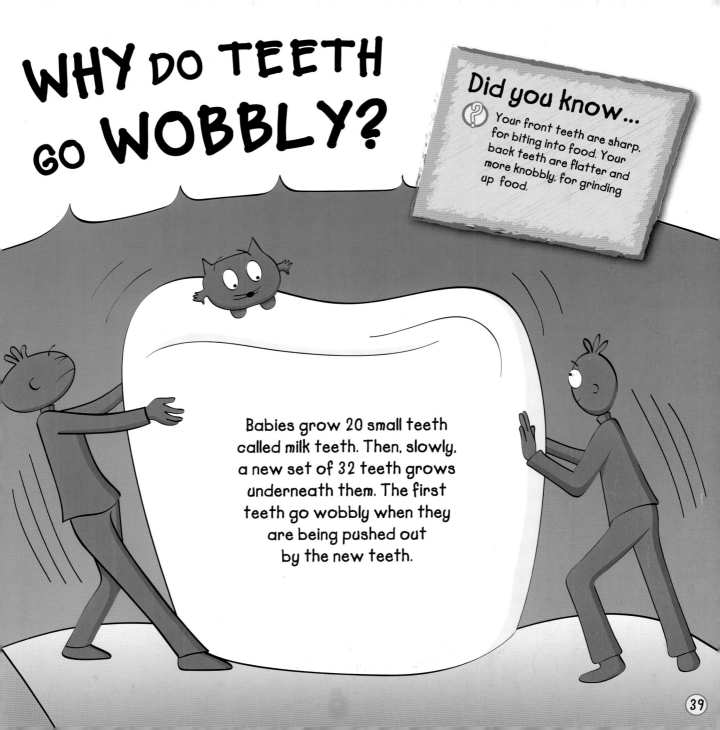

WHY DO I YAWN?

Did you know...

Yawning spreads fast! If one person yawns, anyone who sees them tends to yawn soon afterwards. Nobody knows why.

Nobody knows for certain why we yawn. It could be because we breathe less deeply than normal when we are tired, bored, or just waking up. So, yawning could simply be our body's way of making us breathe better or more deeply.

Z Z Z

WHAT IS SLEEP FOR?

Sleep gives all your body parts a much-needed rest. Without sleep you would soon be too tired and worn-out to even think properly, and you would start to get bad-tempered and clumsy.

Did you know...

Growing up is tiring! Babies sleep for around 14 hours a day. Children need about 10 hours of sleep a day, and adults generally need less.

WHAT AM I DOING WHEN I SLEEP?

Did you know ...

In total, people spend about a third of their lives asleep.

While you are asleep your body relaxes. Your breathing slows down and your heartbeat slows, too. Meanwhile your brain gets the chance to sort and store information from the day. Nobody knows for sure why people dream when asleep. It could be your brain's way of sorting out what you have been thinking.

WHY DO PEOPLE SNORE?

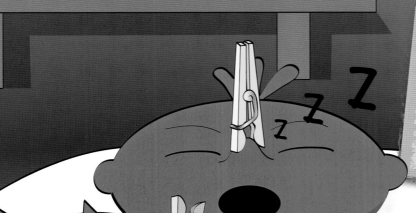

Z Z Z

People may make snoring noises while they sleep, if the back of their throat vibrates (wobbles) in a different way to how it does when they are awake. This might be because someone's nose is blocked up or the back of their throat is slightly blocked.

WHY DOES MY NOSE RUN?

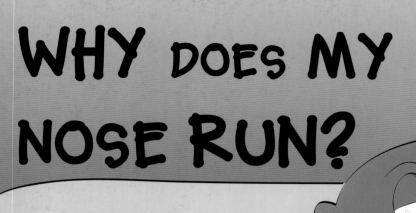

Your nose makes mucus (mew-cus), a gooey slime that is also called snot. It lines the inside of your nose and catches dirt and germs before they get the chance to go into your lungs. Your nose will make extra mucus for protection if it is irritated – perhaps by dust or by the germs you get if you catch a cold.

Did you know...

A nose makes roughly a litre of mucus every day. That's the same as about three or four mugs of snot!

WHAT IS A SNEEZE?

Tiny hairs in your nose help to stop dirt and germs getting in. If they get tickled, perhaps by dust floating in the air, your brain signals to your body to sneeze, to blow the particles out. Your body will try to sneeze out cold germs, too, if you catch a cold.

Did you know...

One sneeze sprays out around 40, 000 tiny liquid droplets from your nose and mouth. This is why it is polite to cover them with your hand or a handkerchief when you sneeze.

ARE ALL BELLY BUTTONS THE SAME?

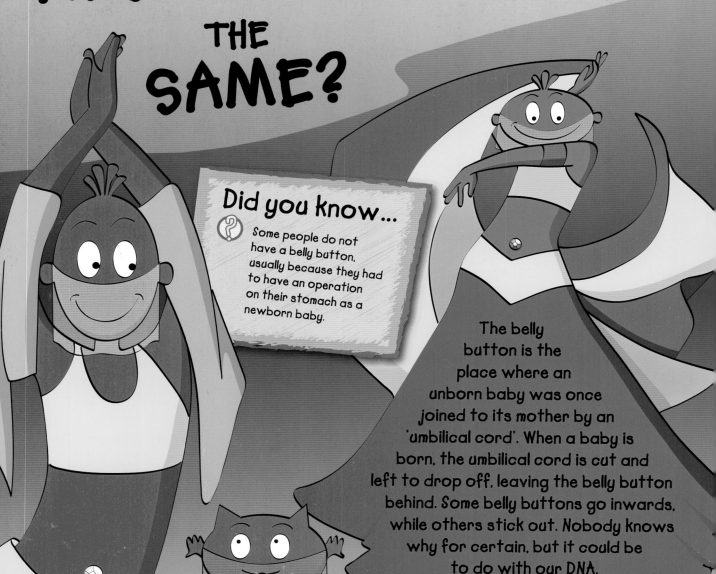

Did you know...

Some people do not have a belly button, usually because they had to have an operation on their stomach as a newborn baby.

The belly button is the place where an unborn baby was once joined to its mother by an 'umbilical cord'. When a baby is born, the umbilical cord is cut and left to drop off, leaving the belly button behind. Some belly buttons go inwards, while others stick out. Nobody knows why for certain, but it could be to do with our DNA.

WHAT MAKES ME HICCUP?

Did you know...

? Even unborn babies can get the hiccups!

Inside your chest, below your lungs, there is a large wall of muscle called your diaphragm (dye-a-fram). It moves up and down automatically when you breathe, but sometimes it gets out of control and this is when you get hiccups. The sound of the hiccup is the noise made by part of your throat closing quickly.

WHY DO SOME PEOPLE WEAR GLASSES?

An eye works by collecting light and focusing it into a picture on the retina – the sensitive layer at the back of your eye. If your eyes cannot focus the light properly, you will not see clearly. Glasses are extra lenses that help eyes to focus better.

Did you know...

Short-sighted people cannot see very far away. Long-sighted people are not able to see things properly when they are close-up.

48

WHAT DOES 'COLOUR BLIND' MEAN?

Colour-blind people cannot tell some colours apart. Inside your eye there are cells called 'cones' that allow you to see different colours. But colour-blind people have some cones that are either missing or not working.

WHY DO I NEED TO GET MY NAILS CUT?

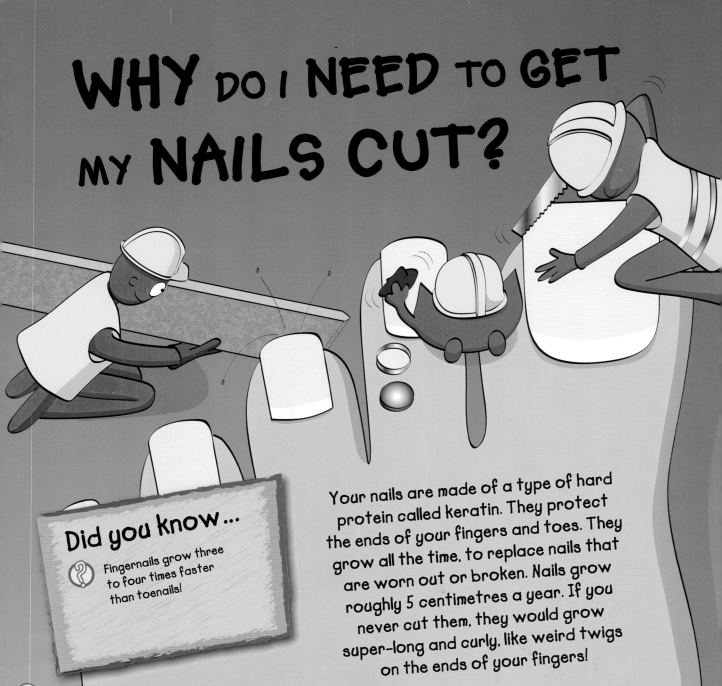

Did you know...

Fingernails grow three to four times faster than toenails!

Your nails are made of a type of hard protein called keratin. They protect the ends of your fingers and toes. They grow all the time, to replace nails that are worn out or broken. Nails grow roughly 5 centimetres a year. If you never cut them, they would grow super-long and curly, like weird twigs on the ends of your fingers!

WHY DOES HAIR FALL OUT?

Did you know...

Hair is made of dead body cells. This is why haircuts do not hurt you.

It is normal to lose between 50 and 100 hairs a day, mostly when you brush or wash your hair. You have about 100,000 hairs on your head. Each hair grows for about two years, from its root inside the skin. When it finally falls out, a new hair grows in its place.

WHY DO EARS MAKE WAX?

Did you know...

The proper name for earwax is 'cerumen' (se-roo-mun).

Your body makes a gooey wax in a tube called the 'ear canal', inside the entrance to your ear. The wax keeps out dirt particles and infections, and stops your ears getting dry and itchy. It is made from body oil, sweat and dead skin flakes. It sounds disgusting, but it does no harm to you. In fact, earwax does a very important job!

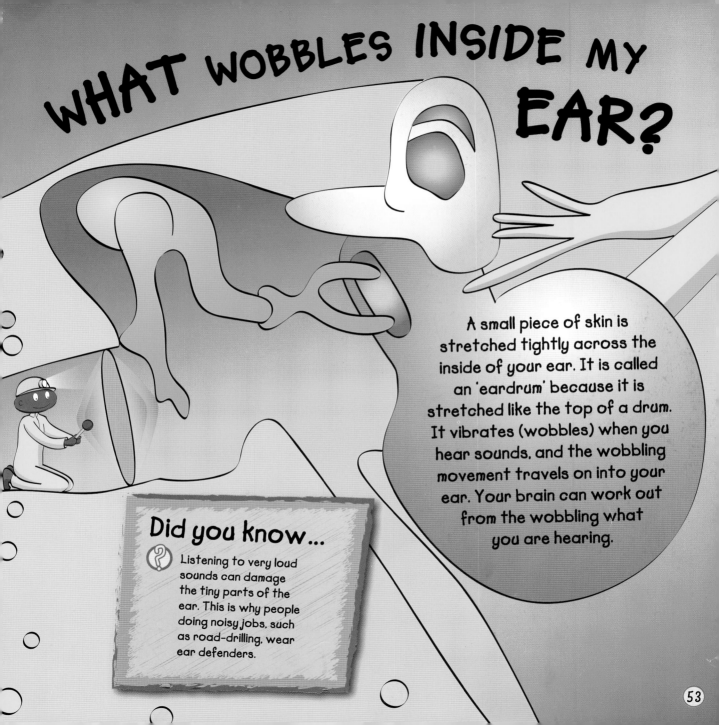

WHAT WOBBLES INSIDE MY EAR?

A small piece of skin is stretched tightly across the inside of your ear. It is called an 'eardrum' because it is stretched like the top of a drum. It vibrates (wobbles) when you hear sounds, and the wobbling movement travels on into your ear. Your brain can work out from the wobbling what you are hearing.

Did you know...

Listening to very loud sounds can damage the tiny parts of the ear. This is why people doing noisy jobs, such as road-drilling, wear ear defenders.

HOW QUICKLY DOES MY HEART BEAT?

When you are resting, your heart beats between 70 and 100 times a minute. The heart is a big muscle that pumps blood around your body. The blood gives you the oxygen you need and takes waste away from your body cells. Your heart beats faster when you exercise, to make sure your body has enough oxygen.

Did you know...

You can feel your heart beating by touching your pulse. Press lightly on the inside of your wrist to feel your blood being pumped around your body. Each beat you feel is your heart contracting (squeezing).

WHY DO I SOMETIMES GET OUT OF BREATH?

When you breathe you take air into your lungs. Here, oxygen from the air passes into your blood, which carries it to all your body cells. When you breathe out you get rid of carbon dioxide, a poisonous gas that your body makes as a waste product. When you exercise, your body cells need more oxygen and make more carbon dioxide. Your lungs work harder, so you breathe more quickly and can feel breathless.

QUICK-QUIZ QUESTIONS

1. How many cells are in your body?
a) thousands b) millions c) trillions

2. Your eyes grow bigger as you get older. True or false?

3. Where would you find a chromogome in your body?

4. Your hair grows faster than anything else on your body. True or false?

5. Do you blink to stop your eyes drying out, or to push away water from your eyes?

6. Name a place on your body where you don't have hair.

7. How much of your body is made of water?

8. The digestive system is the section of the body that makes you breathe. True or false?

9. Does your tummy rumble most when it is empty or full?

10. Do fizzy drinks cure burping?

11. What type of taste do you sense at the front of your tongue – sweet or sour?

12. Your body has lots of thin tubes that carry blood around. What are they called? a) blood ways b) blood vessels c) heart tubes

13. Does your skin have holes in it?

14. Most adults have around 1,000 moles. True or false?

15. Is a lot of sunlight good or bad for the skin?

16. Adults sweat more than children. True or false?

17. Are bones heavy or light?

18. Your bones can rebuild themselves. True or false?

19. Where is your smallest bone?

20. What are a baby's first teeth called?

21. When you are asleep, your breathing slows down. True or false?

22. Do all belly buttons look the same?

23. Colour-blind people cannot see any colours. True or false?

24. What are nails made of?

25. How many times a minute does your heart beat?

QUICK-QUIZ ANSWERS

1. c) trillions
2. False. Your eyes stay the same size all your life.
3. In one of your cells.
4. True.
5. You blink to stop your eye drying out.
6. Soles of feet, palms of hands, eyelids, lips.
7. Two-thirds of your body is water.
8. False. The digestive system processes food.
9. When it is empty.
10. No. Fizzy drinks make burping worse.
11. Sweet.

12. b) blood vessels.

13. Yes – they are called pores.

14. False. Most adults have between 10 and 40 moles.

15. Too much sun is bad for the skin.
16. True.

17. Light.

18. True.

19. In your ear.
20. Milk teeth.

21. True.
22. No. There are 'innies' and 'outies'.

23. False. They cannot tell some colours apart.

24. Nails are made of keratin.
25. Your heart beats between 70 and 100 times a minute.

TRICKY WORDS

BACTERIA

Tiny organisms (life forms), too small to see without a microscope. Some are harmless, but some can make people ill.

BLOOD VESSELS

Narrow tubes that carry your blood around your body.

CARBON DIOXIDE

A gas, poisonous to humans, that is created by your body cells as they do their work.

CELLS

The tiny building blocks that make up every living thing.

CHROMOSOMES

Tiny ladder-shaped threads in every body cell, where DNA is stored.

DIAPHRAGM

A dome-shaped area of muscle that helps you to breathe in and out.

DIGESTIVE SYSTEM

The section of your body that takes the goodness from food and gets rid of any unwanted stuff.

DNA

A set of chemicals found in every cell. DNA controls how the body looks and works.

EAR CANAL

A tube inside the entrance to the ear.

EARDRUM

A tiny piece of skin that is tightly stretched across the inside of the ear.

FEMUR

The biggest bone in the body, located in the top of the leg.

GLAND

A body part that makes a substance, such as earwax, tears or skin oil.

JOINT

The place where two bones meet each other.

LUNGS

Two bag-shaped body parts inside your chest. Air is drawn into the lungs when you inhale (breathe in).

MUCUS

Gooey slime that lines the inside of the nose to catch dirt and infections.

MUSCLE

Stretchy material attached to bones. Muscles contract (squeeze) and relax to make bones move.

NERVE ENDING

A tiny body part that can sense things, such as touch or heat.

OXYGEN

A gas that your body needs to help it work. It is in the air that we breathe in.

PARTICLE

A very tiny piece of something.

PELVIS

A bone in between the base of your back and the top of your legs.

PLATELETS

Cells that float in the blood. Their job is to stop bleeding by clumping together to block cuts.

PORES

Tiny holes all over the skin.

RETINA

The sensitive surface at the back of the eye.

SKELETON

The framework of bones that protects your soft insides and keeps your body shape.

STAPES

The tiniest bone in the body, in the ear.

TASTE BUDS

Tiny spots on your tongue that can sense different types of taste.

UMBILICAL CORD

A cord that attaches an unborn baby to its mother.

URINE

The proper name for wee — water mixed with waste substances that your body needs to get rid of.

VIBRATE

To wobble very rapidly. Parts of the ear vibrate when they hear sounds.

WHERE TO FIND STUFF

B

babies 7, 10, 39, 41, 46, 47

bacteria 31, 60

belly buttons 46

bleeding 22, 23

blinking 10

blood 22, 23, 54

blood vessels 22, 60

bones 6, 32, 33, 35, 36, 37

breathing 40, 42, 55

burping 19

C

carbon dioxide 55, 60

cells 6, 8, 23, 25, 26, 27, 28, 35, 49, 51, 54, 55, 60, 61

chromosomes 8, 60

colour blindness 49

cuts 22, 23, 27

D

diaphragm 47, 60

digestive system 16, 18, 19, 20, 60

DNA 8, 46, 60

dreaming 42

E

eardrum 53, 60

ears 36, 52, 53, 60

earwax 52

eyebrows 12

eyelashes 12

eyelids 10, 11

eyes 7, 10, 11, 12, 48, 49

F

farting 20

femur 37, 60

food 14

freckles 25

G

giggling 30

glands 10, 60

glasses 48

goosebumps 29

H

hair, 9, 13, 51

hearing 36, 53

heart 6, 54

height 9

hiccups 47

hunger 14

JL
joints 33, 34, 60
lungs 55, 60

M
moles 26
mucus 44, 60
muscles 33, 37, 61

N
nails 50
nerves 30, 36, 61
nose 44, 45

O
oil 24, 31, 52
oxygen 54, 55, 61

PQR
pelvis 37, 61
pigment 25, 26
platelets 23, 61
pooing 16
pores 24, 61
prolactin 11
pulse 54
retina 48, 61

S
scabs 23
scars 27
scent 13
shivering 29
skeleton 6, 61
skin 13, 22, 23, 24,
   25, 26, 27, 28, 29
sleeping 41, 42, 43
sneezing 45
snoring 43
stapes 36, 61
stomach 6, 15, 18
sunburn 28
suncream 28
sweat 24, 31, 52

T
taste buds 61
tears 11
teeth 38, 39
thirst 15
tickling 30
tongue 21
tummy 6, 15, 18

U
umbilical cord 46, 61
urine 17, 61

WXYZ
washing 31
water 15
weeing 17
yawning 40

Wow! What an amazing journey! We hope you had as much fun as we did, and learnt many new things. Who knew there was so much to discover about the human body! Here are some other exciting books where you'll find more to explore:

The Book Of... How?
The Book Of... What?
The Book Of... Where?
The Book Of... Which?
The Book Of... Who?
The Book Of... Why?
The Book Of... Dinosaurs

Look out for these great books!
'Who' knows 'what' we'll discover...

See you soon!